BOOK
MARKETING
SECRETS

Paul G. Brodie

DISCLAIMER

The following viewpoints in this book are those of Paul Brodie. These views are based on his personal experience over the past forty-eight years on the planet Earth, especially while living in the great state of Texas.

The intention of this book is to share his story about marketing books successfully and what has worked for *him* through this journey.

All attempts have been made to verify the information provided by this publication. Neither the author nor the publisher assumes any responsibility for errors, omissions, or contrary interpretations of the subject matter herein.

This book is for entertainment purposes only. The views expressed are those of the author alone and should not be taken as expert instruction or commands. The reader is responsible for his or her future action. This book makes no guarantees of future success. However, by following the steps that are listed in this book, the odds of marketing your book successfully have a much higher probability.

Neither the author nor the publisher assumes any responsibility or liability on behalf of the purchaser or reader of these materials.

The views expressed are based on the author's personal experiences within the corporate world, education, and everyday life.

This book is dedicated to my mom, Barbara "Mama" Brodie. Without her support and motivation (and incredible cooking) I would literally not be here today.

I am also dedicating this book to every client I have had the privilege to help grow their business through sharing their story by getting a book published, marketing their book successfully, starting a podcast, or creating and launching a virtual summit.

You have all gone above and beyond chasing your dreams and I am proud to be able to help in your journey.

TABLE OF CONTENTS

FREE BOOK

I would like to offer you the digital version of my *Get Published* book. The brand-new second edition of *Get Published* will only be available on the website for a limited time.

Go to www.BrodieConsultingGroup.com to grab your free copy of *Get Published*.

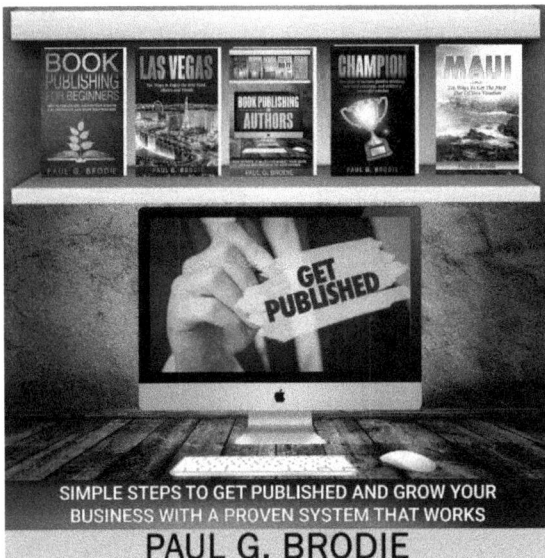

INTRODUCTION

Welcome to my nineteenth book and the third edition of Book Marketing Secrets. This is not your typical how-to book. It's for people who want to know how to market their book effectively and in the most efficient manner possible. This book is for people who want to market their book with a proven system that works. If you want to use your book to build relationships and grow your business, then this book is for you. Marketing your book successfully is one of the best ways to establish authority and be able to sell your services to the warmest leads possible. My company has launched over 100 consecutive books and I will share many of the marketing strategies that we use in this book.

Have you always wanted to have your own best-selling book? Do you find it difficult to know where to start?

I want to tell you that every person can market their book successfully, and this book will help you start with a proven system that works. One of the biggest challenges is just getting started.

The goal is for this book to help you in your journey to market your own book, whether that is by doing it yourself with guidance from our book or by working with us directly through our Done For You (DFY) book launch marketing service and our publishing service.

We will be focusing on not only marketing your book, but also maximizing conversion for book sales and adding readers to your list. There are a lot of pieces that go into a successful book launch, and we'll cover items ranging from building your email list to engaging with your list to converting readers to clients with a simple funnel strategy.

My philosophy in anything I do in life, whether it is teaching, giving motivational seminars, or writing and coaching, is to have the power of one. The power of one is my goal to help at least one person. I hope that person is you.

CHAPTER 1
THREE THINGS YOU MUST HAVE BEFORE LAUNCHING YOUR BOOK

In June 2015, I had an epiphany on a flight to Las Vegas. I decided to finally commit to writing my first book. The next morning, while poolside at The Mirage, I typed the entire outline of the book into my iPhone.

One week later, I wrote the book over a three-day period. Over the next month I found an amazing editor, book formatter, and book cover designer. It was then time to figure out how to market the book.

During July 2015, I attended a virtual summit about publishing, and it was a great help with starting my own author journey. The host interviewed experts from the publishing industry, and I learned about things like book promo companies, launch sequences, affiliate marketing, search engine optimization, using hashtags, finding Facebook groups to promote your book, and other areas.

I felt like I'd just opened a fire hydrant and was hit with a huge blast of water. It was overwhelming, and while I had all these great ideas, I had no clue where to start. First thing I did was to go back to my notes from the summit.

During the summit, I took copious notes. This was before virtual summits offered transcripts and MP3 audio files as part of their VIP/Premium Passes, so I went back to my Word files to reference the notes from the sessions. In all, I had over sixty pages of notes and decided to focus on a few key areas about maximizing conversion for my book.

After watching the sessions and doing Google research, I knew that conversion was the most important thing to start with before I even thought about book launch marketing sequences, book promos, category research, and the other items that go into a successful book launch.

Before you even start a book launch, you must have three key things. If you do not have those items, then you can drive all the traffic you want to the book, but it will not convert into sales nearly as well unless you already have the following.

The first thing you need to have is a great-looking book cover. As a quick tip, go to Amazon and research books like yours in your niche. Look at the sales rankings and go to those pages. Take a close look at those books that are at the top of those categories and think about designing a cover that has some of those elements.

You may also want to think about the branding of your business and connect that with your covers. With my publishing, marketing, and virtual summit books, I always want to make sure they include gold, black, or red as those are the dominant colors in my branding.

This book had a unique design. I wanted the cover to have a mysterious look to it. The cover has a black background with "Book Marketing Secrets" in black with gold behind the title. It reflected my company branding and added an element of intrigue to elicit curiosity.

The second item is having a well-edited and formatted book for both Kindle and paperback. Invest your money in an editor and do not self-edit if you can avoid it. You only get one chance to make a first impression, so invest in a quality editor and a well-formatted book. These are some of the most important investments that you can make in your book.

My company has had the same team of editors, formatters, and book cover designers for years. It is a cohesive team that has one job. That one job is to make sure our clients have the best book possible.

If you want to do this yourself, then find a team. Find editors, formatters, and book cover designers. When you have found the right ones, work with them for all your books. Think of them as some of the best long-term relationships you can have.

The final item is something you want to tackle yourself, and that is the book description. I give our clients a framework and template of how to craft the book description for their sales page on Amazon. We always want the description to be in the author's words because no one knows the book better than the client.

The book description is also known as your sales copy. This is what will help sell your book. The goal of your book description should be to identify a problem that you will help the reader solve.

For my first book, *Eat Less and Move More*, I researched many top authors and looked at their styles. After reading many book descriptions, I came up with the following for *Eat Less and Move More*:

Eat Less and Move More: My Journey shows you how you can change your lifestyle *without spending long hours in the gym and without starving yourself while enjoying cheat meals.*

On May 2, 2011, I received my wake-up call. I was 336 pounds, had borderline type 2 diabetes, and had recently recovered from both bronchitis and pneumonia. My bad eating habits and lifestyle choices were making me ill, but I was too wrapped up in what I was doing to spot the signs, let alone to do anything about it. That day I found myself in the doctor's office and was told that I might not be around in 5-10 years if I didn't change my lifestyle. That was my wake-up call. Luckily I got a second chance.

That day I realized that <u>life is short and precious</u>, and I made a decision that I was going to do things differently. I decided to change my life so that I could live life to the fullest and eat less and move more.

What I decided to create for myself was:

- A healthy lifestyle that I could be proud of
- The mental freedom to live the life of my dreams
- The freedom of good health to do the things I love and to be with the people who matter most to me

And now I want to help you do the same.

After all, deciding to start your journey to eat less and move more is something you do because you have a vision of a better life for you and your family. It's your chance to take control and live life on your terms. And done right, *<u>it will</u> <u>give you</u> the mental freedom and the freedom of good health to do the things you love, when you want to do them and <u>with</u> the peoplewho matter most in your life.*

Eat Less and Move More will show you how to create an improved you that gives you the time to work on your own passions in life. It will also show you the mistakes I made and what I did when I gained over half of the weight back. I also tell my story throughout the book of working in the corporate world and eventually leaving that world to pursue a career in teaching as my weight and career were connected.

In short, losing weight and keeping the weight off is not a temporary change but a lifestyle choice by choosing to <u>eat less and move more.</u>

Eat Less and Move More shows you how you can easily start your own journey toward a healthier lifestyle—a lifestyle that you can be proud of *and* achieve both *mental freedom and freedom of good health.*

But more than this, *Eat Less and Move More* explores what it means to live a truly happy and fulfilled life—to *really live the life of your dreams and pursue what you love.* It encourages you to examine your own motivations and desires in order to determine your path in life.

To get access to the bonus materials and resources (all for FREE), be sure to visit:

<u>www.BrodieEDU.com</u>

It was not bad for my first launch, but I changed my approach for sales copy a few months later and reworked it for *Eat Less and Move More.* I made these changes in late November 2015. One of the best things about Kindle is that you can change and update your book and change your book description whenever you want to.

Here is the new and improved sales copy.

Eat Less and Move More: My Journey shows how you can change your mindset and improve your physical and mental health.

What if a few new habits could improve your personal health? What if you could increase your health and happiness with a few simple steps? Imagine waking up in the morning feeling healthy and happy and ready to take on the day.

Amazon bestselling author, Paul G. Brodie, in his first book, covers multiple ways to improve your physical and mental health.

Here are a few things that you will get out of *Eat Less and Move More*.In this book, you will learn:

- How to learn to listen to your body
- How to take a leap of faith and follow your dreams
- How to respond when your body gives you a wake up call
- How to eat less and move more
- How to respond if you gain weight after an initial weight loss
- How to create a healthy environment by eating clean
- How to change your lifestyle at any age
- How to utilize healthy eating habits in your everyday life

- How to enjoy cheat meals without feeling guilty
- BONUS: Daily food lists for what Paul has utilized to lose over sixty pounds, plus current food items that he eats to continue to live a healthy lifestyle

Buy this book NOW to increase your personal, physical, and mental health

Pick up your copy today by clicking the BUY NOW button at the top of this page!

As you can see, I made a much better effort in identifying a problem for the reader and offering solutions. In addition, I added two calls to action at the end of the sales copy by telling the reader to buy now. Calls to action may sound basic, but they do work.

When you write your book description, remember that the first sentence you write is the big promise. This is what the reader will get out of your book. With *Eat Less and Move More*, the first sentence was "change your mindset and improve your physical and mental health."

Once you have written your first sentence with the big promise, you'll want to follow with two additional benefits of buying your book. Using "what if" and "imagine" statements are great ways to introduce the two additional benefits.

The book description needs to explain the content of your book with benefits to the reader. Another thing you can do is offer bonuses in the description. In my Maui books, I offer a free travel guide as one of the bonuses.

As you approach the end of your book description, you want to restate the big promise again. With *Eat Less and Move More* I added "buy this book NOW to increase your personal physical and mental health."

At the end of the book description, you want to close with BUY NOW. Here is how I close *Eat Less and Move More*: Pick up your copy today by clicking the BUY NOW button at the top of this page!

Once you have completed your sales copy, the next step is to have it converted to HTML so your book description will stand out. With HTML you can bold and highlight words, increase font size, and underline words. You can use a free book description generator on www.kindlepreneur.com that will automatically convert your text into HTML code.

CHAPTER 2
OPTIMIZING
YOUR BOOK

The other area of optimization is inside your book. When you launch a book, you are most likely starting either with a small audience or no audience at all. One of the main things you want to do is to have as many of those readers as possible sign up for your email list.

You can get a free account with Mailchimp as your CRM (Customer Relationship Management) as you can have your first 2,000 subscribers on their service for free. I cannot emphasize how important it is to build your email list, and we will talk more about that later in this book.

To be able to build your list, you must give something of value in exchange for the reader to give you their email address. In the front of this book, you are presented with an offer to grab a free digital copy of my *Get Published* book. Since 2018, I have offered that lead magnet on my website as well as with my Get Published Summit and with my other books. That offer alone has added over 3,000 readers to my email list. Having an offer in the first section of your book as part of the front matter is critical. I do cover this more in depth in *Get Published* and you can grab your free copy at www.BrodieConsultingGroup.com.

The second thing you need is a website. It doesn't have to be the world's greatest website, but I do recommend that you have a few things on it. My website started with a basic front page that had our old company logo, some information about me and the business, and the offer to grab a free copy of my *Get Published* book.

Over the past five years the website has evolved into a full eCommerce site. When you go to www.BrodieConsultingGroup.com the first thing you see our office image. On the left side of the website is a series of tabs offering links and details about who we are, services, a free book, info about our Get Published Podcast, a media page for how shows can book me and examples of shows I have been on, info about our virtual summit service, and a link to our Facebook group. Below the tabs is an invitation to set up a complimentary strategy session with me along with my email address, and also links to connect with our Get Published Facebook Group and to connect with my on LinkedIn where I have over 10,000 connections.

Those areas have a lot of info and give people multiple ways to connect with me. As you scroll down the webpage, you see several stats, from the number of downloads to how we have launched over one hundred best-selling books. Below that area we have a section about our core values; as you scroll down the page, you then see a one-minute explainer video that gives more info about how we help. You also see a client testimonials area, a client collage with their pictures and books, a testimonial video from one of our clients, some info about me, another opportunity to set up a strategy session, and another chance to grab a free copy of *Get Published*.

The other thing I have on the site is a chat bot from HubSpot. The free chat program invites readers to connect with us and to potentially set up a strategy session to learn more about how we help. Every part of our website is set up for conversion.

I wanted to share this because the main thing is to get a website up and running. Over time, you can make the upgrades and improvements. It's very important to offer something of value in exchange for the reader's email address. You will also need a program to house the free book. I have used Leadpages since 2015 and I use them for all my lead magnets.

For the strategy session offer, you can get a free account on Calendly where people can book their call with you. On your website, you can have the strategy session invitation link connect to Calendly—it's a quick and easy way for readers to schedule a call with you.

You also want to have a strategy session offer at the end of your book. After the conclusion of this book, you are given an invitation to set up a complimentary strategy session with me. It's a no-pitch session where we talk about your potential book to see how we can help. You always want to make clear it is a no-pitch session, and the goal is to see how you can help. By having this mindset, you will be amazed at how great many of those calls can be as they set potential clients at ease, knowing it is a conversation and not a pitch fest.

I had a call with a potential client a few hours before I wrote this chapter. She mentioned that she was being hounded by multiple hybrid publishers who wanted to publish her book. I told her immediately that she will never get a call like that from my company.

The main reason is because we do not pitch or push our services. Our traffic is generated from those who read our books, attend our virtual summits (our annual Get Published Summit and Platform Building Summit) and through my Get Published Podcast and the shows that I serve as a guest on. I also mentioned that a lot of our clients refer business to us because we have learned that taking care of clients and getting great results for them is the best marketing you can do. Our clients are by far the best people to promote us.

A great example is our clients Sheriff Mark Lamb and his wife, Janel. Mark and Janel reached out to me after Janel heard me on the Intermittent Fasting Stories Podcast with my friend Gin Stephens. During the show, I spoke about my own health and wellness journey with intermittent fasting and about how I help people share their story.

After the call with Mark and Janel, they both became clients. We had the privilege of helping them successfully publish four books, and all four became huge hits and #1 best sellers in multiple categories. They both also have large social media audiences, so we were able to use our own launch sequence and then leverage their followings, and the results were amazing.

Mark and Janel not only are wonderful clients but also became great friends of mine. I refer to Mark as a brother because of the connection we made, and we look forward to helping him with many more books in the future. Mark also has referred multiple people to us who have become clients; taking great care of your clients is the best way to market your business in my view.

CHAPTER 3
BUILDING YOUR
EMAIL LIST

As I mentioned in chapter 2, building your email list as soon as possible is critical. To this day it blows my mind when I talk with prospective clients about their books, especially those who have already published and launched several books, and they tell me they do not have an email list.

I always ask why they have not built a list and the typical answer is that Amazon keeps their lists of people who buy their books. At that point, I explain how Amazon works and that you have to get those readers to your lists by offering something of value in exchange for their email address. Amazon does not share the contact information of people who buy your book, which is why you must have a lead magnet in the book to get people to subscribe to your email list in exchange for something of value.

It can be a checklist, eBook, guide, first chapter of your next book, a previous book, etc. This offer should be in the front matter of every book you publish. This is a method I've embraced since watching that publishing summit in 2015. When I watched several of those summit interviews, the guests brought up multiple times the importance of having your own list and getting as many readers as possible to that list.

I did that with my first book and have done so for the other eighteen, including this one. You also want to have the lead magnet on your website. Our *Get Published* book brought in over 3,000 new readers to my email list with that one offer.

The other thing is to always make an offer if you are on podcasts, blogs, or other shows. Usually at the end of an interview, the host will ask where people can go to get more information about you. This is a great opportunity to promote your offer to their audience. I always answer by mentioning that the audience can grab a free digital copy of my Get Published book at www.BrodieConsultingGroup.com. In addition, they can book a complimentary no-pitch strategy session with me to talk about their book and can also check out our Get Published Podcast on the site.

The main thing I am doing is emphasizing value, value, and more value. If they go to my site, they can grab a free book, listen to my free podcast, or set up a complimentary session with me to talk about their book. This strategy has brought in hundreds of thousands of dollars to my business.

The most important part about having your own email list is that you control it. If you are on any social media platforms such as Facebook, everything can change within a day. Facebook has been known to change their algorithms constantly, and if you're relying on organic traffic on social media, you may want to reconsider focusing mainly on social media. The same goes for Instagram and Pinterest—everything can change in an instant because they control the traffic.

When you have your own list, you control the traffic. It cannot be changed on a whim by Mark Zuckerberg. I have witnessed authors who had Facebook pages that once were able to reach tens of thousands of people become a ghost town, all because of a change in their algorithm. This is why you must have your own list.

Having your own traffic is critical, and the best way to do that is with your own email list. It can never be taken away from you since those subscribers opted in and cannot be changed based on an algorithm shift.

CHAPTER 4
ENGAGING WITH
YOUR EMAIL LIST

O nce you start to build your email list, you'll want to engage with your subscribers. You can ask one hundred authors with email lists the best way to engage with those lists, and you will most likely receive one hundred different answers. The main thing is that engagement is critical and you need to figure out the communication rhythm that fits you and your schedule the best.

I will share with you what has worked for me, as we tend to market a little differently compared to others. The first thing you want to consider is how often should you email your list. My friend and fellow author, Derek Doepker, emails his list roughly five times per week. The emails are a mix of storytelling and affiliate offers. Derek is one of the best when it comes to writing emails, and I would recommend checking out his website and joining his list to see how he does it.

Derek has been a guest on several of my summits, and our Get Published Summit interview this year focused on how he engages with his list. In the interview, he shares several of his favorite tactics for engagement and for including affiliate promos. The affiliate promos can add an extra four figures in monthly revenue to your business.

In March, April, and May of 2021, I ran three affiliate promos. One was for Alinka Rutkowska's multi-author book, which guaranteed that the book would be on the *USA Today* best-sellers list. The second promo was with Matt Stone for his 100 Covers service, and the third was with Derek for his Audiobooks Made Easy course.

All three people are friends of mine, have been frequent collaborators, and have products that I believe in and personally vouch for. Each of those promos made us four figures. This is something that I do not recommend doing until you have spent time (usually a few months) engaging with your list.

Make sure that when you do start to do affiliate promos, they are with people who you have gotten to know and have products that are great products and will help get your readers an outcome they are looking for. I cannot emphasize how important this is because by vouching for the affiliates, you are not only endorsing them, you are also putting your business reputation on the line.

I did several more affiliate promos in the fall of 2021 and each continued to bring in four figures. During the spring and summer of 2022 and 2023, I have already scheduled four more affiliate promos as they are a great source of revenue. Again, I suggest being selective with who you do these promos with, but once you find the right fit then it can be mutually beneficial while providing additional value to your audience.

In 2023, the promos we did with Derek and Matt became even bigger successes as my list has grown quite a lot since 2022. We ended up getting triple the sales so it shows that you can run affiliate promotions with each affiliate at least 1-2 times a year and also increase revenue from those promotions as long as you are working to grow your list and also engage with your list at least once a week.

By engaging with your email list, your readers are getting to know, like, and trust you, and you are building a potential long-term relationship. They will be the ones who buy your services, purchase affiliate products that you promote, buy your books, and are your core audience. I have had people on my list who have been there since 2015 and still engage with me.

In terms of how often you should email your list, I'll share what I do. Every Tuesday at 9:15 a.m. Central Time, I have a weekly email that is sent to my list. I structure the email first with a story, then I provide an update of what I'm working on, which is usually an upcoming book or virtual summit. I may also share the results of a book launch we're doing for a client. I include a home improvement update, as I have been working on multiple projects, from building my home retro arcade (took over six months) to my backyard barbecue area and even man cave updates.

When you start your email with a story, do not be afraid to be vulnerable. In July 2021, my 13-year-old German Shepherd, Athena, passed away suddenly, and I shared that story.

In August 2021, I adopted a Golden Retriever puppy and named her Amaris. In each weekly email, I added an Amaris update as sharing the story of losing my dog and then adopting a new puppy resonated with my audience and we received a lot of positive feedback. My audience has received updates and funny stories about Amaris as a puppy and we always get great responses. Being vulnerable creates a deeper connection between you and your reader and can be applied in emails, books, and other content.

In January 2022, I got a bad case of COVID and it attacked my lungs. It put me out of commission for two weeks as I have a previous history of bronchitis and pneumonia. I shared that story with my audience and my road to recovery. After that email, I received many messages of support, and it was another great opportunity to build a stronger connection with my audience.

I also share a book club segment that covers the book I'm currently reading. At the end of that section, I ask if they have any books they recommend I check out. Every week, I get at least one or two book recommendations. I did have to add that I am looking for recommendations of books from other authors as several readers kept pitching me their own books. There is a podcast update segment where readers can subscribe to my Get Published Podcast, and then I wrap up the email.

Every email I write ends with my name followed by the super signature. The super signature was created by internet marketing expert Dean Jackson. It's one of the most powerful tools you have when writing emails.

That section with the super signature will say the following:

P.S. Whenever you're ready, here are three ways we can help in your author journey. The first option is to book your complimentary marketing session this week, and we include the Calendly booking link where the reader can book the session directly. The second gives them an option to book a complimentary publishing strategy session with the Calendly booking link. The third option is an invitation to join our Get Published Facebook group.

Those options are at the bottom of each email I send out to my list. Every week, I have readers who book strategy sessions with me. We have also added over 1300 members to our Get Published Facebook group. I am still not a huge fan of social media, but I do like having the group as an additional avenue for readers to connect with me. However, our core business for our readership will always be our email list.

In addition to the weekly emails, I also send other emails when we are promoting an affiliate offer or when I'm hosting either the Get Published Summit or Platform Building Summit. If I am guest on another virtual summit then I will also send emails to promote that summit as well as a speaker affiliate. Those can be an additional three or four emails during that week.

This is also why I like to send one weekly email most of the time. That way you don't burn out your list, and then subscribers know that when I'm promoting something, it is usually going to be something that will help them. It's also important to note that you want to pick and choose the affiliate promos carefully so that you don't do them more than once per month, as we have found that method to work best.

I also want to share a bonus strategy created by Dean Jackson. It's called the nine-word email, another powerful tool that can convert readers into clients. The nine-word email is perfect for when you want get a lot of responses from your email list quickly. It is a simple strategy and one I only recommend using every three to six months. If you want to use it, this is what you need to do.

First think up a creative subject for the email. Several tactics have been used for the nine-word email, and you could use the first name shortcode in your CRM. That way, every reader sees an email with their name as the subject. That can work, but I would rotate it with other subject lines the next time you use it to keep it fresh. Other examples of subjects could be catching up, here you go, three things, etc.

Once you've come up with your subject, it's time to create a short email. In the email, you can write the following: "Are you still interested in working together?" or "Would you like to work together to...?"

Now, I didn't use nine full words as examples because I wanted to show you the framework. Here is one I have used with my list: "Are you still interested in getting your book published?"

Those nine words equaled 150 responses, twenty strategy sessions, and several new clients. It is a powerful tactic and is something I would recommend testing at least three months after you start building your email list. Again, the main thing you want to do at first is build a relationship with your audience so they get to know, like, and trust you.

If you already have a decent-sized list, then feel free to try it out and let me know how it went. We are always testing new strategies, and the super signature and nine-word email are tactics we have used to great effect since 2017. They both work well as long as they're done correctly.

There is one final piece about engagement, and that is what to do with those on your list who are not engaging with your emails. On Mailchimp, each reader is given a star rating ranging from five stars for the most engaged to one star for the least engaged. The five and four-star readers are the ones who read most if not all emails and click on the links in the emails, ranging from subscribing to my podcast and booking a strategy session to buying products from affiliates. Your three-star readers are the ones who sometimes read the emails. The two-star and one-star readers are not reading the emails and are taking up space on your list.

I tend to delete subscribers from my list every three months. It is my own version of a purge, but with email addresses. If I have subscribers who are at one or two stars, then I give them three months, and if they're still at those same ratings, I remove them. I have deleted over fifteen thousand email subscribers from my list since starting my own journey in 2015.

My email list is currently over 6,000 and over 3,500 of those readers are five and four stars with an additional 750 at three stars. The rest are on the chopping block—I would much rather have an engaged list, as size does not matter when it comes to your email list. Do not be afraid to remove readers from your list if they're not engaged with you.

What matters is that the people on your list are engaged and enjoy your emails. Services like Mailchimp and others can be anywhere from fifty dollars to three hundred dollars per month. I want to keep my costs down, as the last thing you want is to pay for people who are not engaged with you.

CHAPTER 5
DOES SOCIAL
MEDIA HELP?

This chapter may be the most polarizing chapter in this book. Some people swear by social media and how you can build your own little empire on it. I respectfully disagree.

Ten years ago, you may have been able to do this. The problem these days is that social media is highly polarizing with all the political chatter you see on it. Social media companies like Facebook and Instagram also want you to pay for the privilege and use their paid advertising to reach your audience.

Going viral, while not impossible, is harder than ever. In my view, social media is great for awareness. It is not great for conversion. Let me give you an example.

This year at the Get Published Summit, one hundred percent of my speakers promoted the event via email. Last year, ninety percent of our speakers promoted the event. Of that ninety percent, three of those speakers only promoted on social media. They had a combined Facebook following of roughly three hundred thousand. All three did several posts to their audience to promote the summit.

Their hard work resulted in 120 attendees and two premium pass sales. In comparison, the rest of our speakers promoted to their email lists and resulted in 3,350 attendees and 201 premium pass sales. This is just one example of the power of having your own list compared to social media. In 2023, I made it clear that all speakers had to send two emails to their list and they all did so.

By getting all the speakers to promote to their email lists, it resulted in the following results. We generated $14,000 in premium pass sales, had 3502 people attend, and made over five figures after the event with our live webinar that helped sell our done for you book publishing service and our done for you book launch marketing service.

I hear clients all the time worrying about having a Facebook author page, an Instagram account, a Twitter account, and other social media. The main advice I give them is to focus on creating a quality lead magnet, having a website built, and starting to build their own email list. Those three areas are what will convert.

Again, social media is great for awareness, but from what I have witnessed over the years, it's not ideal for conversion. I will mention one social media outlet I have used to great success, and that is LinkedIn.

We have recruited over ninety-five percent of our podcast guests from LinkedIn. If you were to consider any social media outlet, I would highly recommend looking into LinkedIn. We have been able to build our LinkedIn following to over ten thousand followers.

A tactic we used was a program called Meet Alfred. We used it to book guests for the podcast and also to connect with influencers. The program works with LinkedIn Sales Navigator. In Sales Navigator you can use Meet Alfred for search options and search for people you feel would be a great fit for your book. You could use it to send a lead magnet. We used it to invite people in our target market to be a guest on our podcast as long as they either had published a book or were currently writing their book. You can use Meet Alfred together with LinkedIn Sales Navigator to send connection requests for up to two hundred people per day. It's worth checking out if you want to build a LinkedIn following; quite frankly, that is the only social media outlet I've seen a great return on.

Using Meet Alfred with LinkedIn Sales Navigator grew my following to over ten thousand on LinkedIn and brought in podcast guests, leads, clients, and most importantly, life-changing sales revenue.

CHAPTER 6
CREATING A
BOOK LAUNCH
MARKETING PLAN

There is an old phrase that basically says that if you fail to plan, then you plan to fail. When I figured out the editing, formatting, and book cover areas for my first book, I knew I would need to not only come up with a book launch plan, but I would need to invest in marketing.

At the time, I was still a teacher and I made enough money to pay the bills but didn't have much left over every month. My monthly budget was tight and it was tough to put much money together for new projects. Once I wrote my book, I knew I would need money for the editing, formatting, book cover, and especially the book launch.

I told my dad about the book and my struggles, and he lent me two thousand dollars so I could get the book out in the world and have funds to invest in marketing. After researching book launch marketing and Facebook author groups, I knew that investment would be key.

You only get one chance to make a first impression, and I knew I would need to invest in marketing—I have seen this is one of the main reasons that most authors fail to successfully launch their books. They do not invest in marketing, and that is one of the most critical things to do when you market a book. You have to spend money to make money.

While the virtual summit I attended was helpful, I only learned about two book promo companies during the summit: Freebooksy and Buck Books. Both book promo companies are still going strong, and we use both as part of our book launch marketing system. I also learned that social media, as discussed in the last chapter, is great for awareness but not as much for conversion.

In addition, I learned about how Amazon KDP Select works. If the Kindle version of your book is enrolled in Amazon KDP Select, then the book is exclusive to Amazon. One of the great benefits about this is that you can price your Kindle at free for up to five days for your launch. This is part of our book launch marketing system and we still use all five free days because they work.

We have tested many variances with our book launch and this is what we have found to be the most effective. Have your book enrolled in Amazon KDP Select for the first ninety days.

You can then remove your book from Amazon KDP Select after the first ninety days if you want to.

The reason we want the books to be free for five days is because your book will generate potentially thousands of free Kindle downloads during that time. This is part of how the Amazon algorithm works, as it tracks both free and paid downloads for your launch. It also gets your Kindle version into as many hands as possible, and those people may become future clients.

For the 99 cent paid phase, we have changed this strategy several times over the past two years. Starting in 2023, we now use the following strategy. On day six of the launch once the initial five-day free phase period is completed then we take a one day break between the free phase and the 99 cent phase.

We do this so that Amazon has a one-day break to reset their rankings from the free categories to the paid categories. It also helps with any potential sales ranking delays. By this point, our clients typically average between 1000 to 4000 downloads during the free phase of the launch. On day seven we begin the paid phase of the launch with stacking multiple book promos on day seven and also on day eight. We focus on those two days to get at least the first 40-60 sales. This is to ensure you are able to generate enough downloads to hit #1 in at least one category for the best-selling author piece.

With Amazon having issues with sales rankings literally falling off a cliff after a couple days, we also focus on getting additional sales for the next week. Our clients typically get between 120-150 paid sales during the paid phase of the launch and we like to spread out those sales for roughly a one week period.

One of the questions we get often is when the book should be uploaded. When we do launches for clients, we have two weeks for the launch sequence. Those weeks are the upload week and online launch week.

During the first week, which is upload week, we upload the Kindle version of the book on Monday. Typically, Amazon will contact us within two to four hours to let us know the book is now available on Amazon. At that point we send the link to our client and ask them to get five book reviews.

The client getting five reviews as soon as possible is an important part of our process because several of the main book promo companies we use require at least five reviews prior to running the scheduled promo. As a publisher, it's against Amazon's terms of service to offer reviews, but we do show our clients several ways to get those reviews.

The first option is to send out advance review copies of your book electronically via email to people who have agreed to read your book. Just realize that people get busy, and you'll need to reach out to at least twenty-five to fifty people to ensure you have enough reviews. With my first book, I reached out to over 150 people. They were friends, family, and people in my network. All those people resulted in twelve reviews, so be persistent in getting those reviews. It can be a struggle, especially with this being your first or second book, and persistence is the key.

The second option is to find a review service. There's only one I recommend: Pubby. They offer a service where you pay roughly twenty dollars per month and then you earn what is called snaps. Think of snaps like currency that you can use to get others to review your book. You start with two thousand snaps when you sign up, though keep in mind that they do offer a free trial.

You earn snaps by reviewing other people's books who are on Pubby. Typically, you earn between one thousand and two thousand snaps for every book you review. Books range from downloading a copy for free and then leaving an Amazon review to buying a Kindle copy of a book at either $0.99, $1.99, or $2.99. The more expensive the book is, the more snaps you earn. The site is www.Pubby.co if you want to sign up for a free trial.

When I launched *Virtual Summit Secrets*, I was able to get over forty reviews within a two-month period. It is well worth checking out if you need help getting reviews. Those first five reviews are critical, so make sure you have a process to get them as soon as possible.

This is also why we have the upload week—so that our clients can get those reviews and we are also able to get the paperback version of the book approved, which can take a few days. The paperback version sometimes is not approved due to a paperback book cover issue and you have to adjust the size of the paperback cover.

This is why publishing your book yourself can be a rough process, especially if Amazon is being picky approving your book cover. We sometimes have that happen with our own uploads and we are able to get it resolved within twenty-four hours.

During upload week, you get five reviews and the Kindle and paperback versions of your book uploaded and approved. I highly recommend always having both a Kindle and paperback version for your book regardless of genre. The final thing to do is make sure everything looks good on your Amazon page from the book description to the cover, and confirm that your book is in the correct book categories.

During the online launch week, we are now on week #2. We want to officially start the launch on Wednesday of the week. The Kindle version of your book is free from Wednesday through Sunday and then priced at 99 cents during the paid phase of the book launch.

Since 2015, we have tested multiple launch sequences, and this one is what we have found works best. You have the Kindle version of your book free for five days and then one final push on day six and day seven at 99 cents to hit #1 in at least one category on the paid side.

With our client launches, we use over twenty different book promo companies that we have used since starting out in

2015. All the book promo companies have been tested over time, and we have created a sequence where we are able to maximize the results for our clients. The book launch marketing system we have created has resulted in over one hundred consecutive successful best-selling book launches for our clients.

Another area that is critical to the success of your book launch is choosing the best book categories, and we will discuss category research later in this book.

We'll also cover two other things to do when your book launch is wrapping up. The first one is to create a press release once your book has hit #1. The second thing is to plan a podcast tour. We will cover both later in this book.

CHAPTER 7
BOOK PROMO
COMPANIES

In the previous chapter, I mentioned two book promo companies. Both are companies that we use for every book launch. Freebooksy is one of the best book promo companies to use when your book is going through the free phase. They will typically bring in anywhere from five hundred to four thousand free downloads.

Freebooksy will help you with those downloads on the day you use them, and you will typically get some additional downloads on the following day as well. For the free phase, I highly recommend using them. You will need to figure out which day will work best for you during the free phase. We usually book them for the second or fourth day of this phase.

Another great book promo company to consider during the free phase of your launch is The Fussy Librarian. They are often booked weeks in advance, so make sure to book them the moment your book is available. Booking promos as quickly as possible will help get your book promos added to the schedule.

During the paid phase, you want to stack as many promos as possible. Buck Books is just one great site we use. Matt Stone is the owner of Buck Books and has been a friend of mine for years. He has been on our virtual summits, and we did an affiliate promo with his book cover service at 100 Covers. We use Buck Books for every launch when we enter the 99-cent phase. They always help us get the results we're looking for.

Another company to consider is kBook Promotions as their service is a great option to consider. They have been around for a while and they help get results for your book. A few more to consider are Reading Deals, Robin Reads, Bargain Booksy, Awesome Gang, and Book Zio for when your Kindle book is 99 cents (or $1.99 if a Children's Book) for that day.

Our publishing company has launched over one hundred books, all of which hit #1 in at least one category. The main reason for this is because we have a proven system that works, plus we invest significant funds in paid advertising to maximize conversion with book promo companies and to ensure our clients get the results they want. The best part about book promo companies is that they have lists ranging from ten thousand subscribers to over one hundred and fifty thousand subscribers. They either promote free books or discounted books (99 cents). Those companies send a daily email to their list promoting those books.

In other words, the book promos go straight to the reader's email address. They are not on a social media site hoping that the potential reader may see the book and possibly download a copy. Instead, they are sending emails to readers who have opted into their lists. The readers enjoy receiving the emails and are much more likely to buy one of the books listed in that day's email blast.

This is similar to when you have your own email list, and you own the traffic; the same thing goes for the book promo companies. This helps maximize conversion. All the reader must do is open the email, look at the free or discounted book, and then get one of the books. The books are listed in the email and usually include the book cover, so all the reader needs to do is click on the link to be taken to Amazon to buy a copy of your book.

This is why we mainly focus on paid advertising for our clients' books, as results are the key. There are many other book companies to research. When I was looking at book promo companies back in 2015 with my own book, there were many different companies.

The landscape has changed over the years and results do vary. There has been a lot of changeover with book promo companies—some companies have gone out of business and new companies have emerged. One of the other challenges is to be able to get the book promo for your launch day. Fortunately, we have established relationships with several of the top book promo companies and are able to email them directly a few weeks prior to get our clients added to the schedule. This did not happen overnight, and it took years of bookings to build these relationships.

Book promo companies will be the best way for you to get the results you are looking for. In the next chapter, we will cover how to find book categories to help ensure you hit #1 in at least one category for the best-selling author piece.

CHAPTER 8
HITTING BEST-SELLER AND CATEGORY RESEARCH

O ne of the most critical parts of marketing your book launch successfully to become a best-seller is choosing the right book categories. To hit #1, not only do you have to invest in marketing your book, but you also must make sure your book is in the right categories so that it has every chance to hit #1 in at least one category. There are over nineteen thousand book categories on Amazon so the research can be extensive. My company has a list of over four hundred categories we use for our clients' book launches. One tip I want to share is how to choose the best categories for your book.

On June 1, 2023, there was a huge change with Amazon KDP. Amazon is now allowing you to choose three categories when you upload your book. You are no longer able to ask for your book to be in any additional categories for new books. If your book is already on Amazon, then you are able to keep it in its current categories. However, if you change any of the categories in the future then Amazon KDP does state they will remove the other categories that your book is in. The good news is that they have transferred most of the categories they have into the new category selection option so it is not bad as expected. This is why finding the best categories for your book is critical as you now only have three categories to choose from.

There is a program we use called Publisher Rocket that was created by my friend, Dave Chesson. Dave was on the Get Published Summit previously and we took a deep dive into Publisher Rocket and some of the other tech he has created for authors.

You can get more information about Publisher Rocket at www.Kindlepreneur.com; Dave has a lot of great resources for authors. Publisher Rocket currently costs ninety-seven dollars and may be one of the best investments you can make for your author journey. The software lets you research over nineteen thousand Amazon categories for your book in all genres.

We have mainly used Publisher Rocket for the four hundred categories we use for our clients. It does take a lot of time and patience to research the different categories. One of the biggest challenges is to make sure you choose categories that generate traffic and are in your niche.

In other words, you do not want to have the top book in the underwater basket-weaving category for your nonfiction business book. There is not an actual underwater basket-weaving category, but I wanted to use that as a somewhat extreme example.

One of the categories that we like to use for all genres is electronic publishing. The good news is that you can select electronic publishing manually with the new category selection process that started on June 1, 2023. One thing I do suggest is that you put the names of the three categories that you choose into your keywords when you are choosing your book categories in the Kindle eBook details section when you are either uploading the Kindle version of your book or when you are updating the categories.

You do not have to enter the entire category path. As an example, the full path for electronic publishing is Kindle Store > Kindle eBooks > Computers & Technology > Tech Culture & Computer Literacy > Electronic Publishing. You do not need to use that entire path. Instead, all you need to do is enter electronic publishing as the keyword. This will help protect you against any audits that Amazon may do with your categories.

I also recommend deciding on your final categories two days before your book launch is scheduled to start. You can update your categories at any time by going into the Kindle version of your book, selecting the new categories, and then publishing the Kindle again. It will usually take a few hours to update the newly selected categories on Amazon.

The reason I recommend that is because Amazon's audits usually take a few weeks from when the book is uploaded, so this will protect you in case an issue arises. Amazon removed my Book Publishing for Beginners book from a category called book publishing, which is quite comical. They have no rhyme or reason in their audits so make sure to protect yourself in case an audit happens to your book.

We have studied Amazon book categories since 2015 and the categories do change, as does their processes as evident from the new category rules. Our publishing company is constantly keeping on top of any Amazon trends with their algorithm and with the categories, as they have been known to make adjustments consistently. If you are looking to find categories yourself, one of the best options is Publisher Rocket.

In Publisher Rocket, you can click on category search and use their search engine to type in keywords to help you find the categories you are looking for. Select eBook and then type in a word related to your book. As an example, I just typed "marketing" in the search engine and thirty book categories showed up.

You are then presented with four different areas to help you choose the best category. The one you want to focus on is sales to #1. This is not always completely accurate, and they offer a link to click on to see the current #1 book in that category on Amazon. As an example, I found the following category path: Kindle Store > Kindle eBooks > Business & Money > Industries >

Nonprofit Organizations & Charities > Marketing & Communications. I then clicked on the link to see the current #1 book in the category.

After clicking on the "check it out" link, I found that The Undefeated Marketing System was the #1 book. I clicked on the book link to see the overall ranking and the category ranking. The book was currently #1 in two categories and the overall sales ranking was 42,000. This is a great category, so I copied the category path Kindle Store > Kindle eBooks > Business & Money > Industries > Nonprofit Organizations & Charities > Marketing & Communications and then pasted it in a Word file to use later for when I want to update my categories.

You can also do a Google search on book categories as another option, plus I like to research book categories directly on Amazon. I will search for books in the Kindle store and then scroll down to see the book sales rankings for both the book category and overall category. Ideally you want to find that the #1 book has a sales ranking between 10,000 and 55,000 overall.

This is because those categories are driving traffic. They are not the most highly competitive categories, but they are in your genre. Again, you do not want to be #1 in underwater basket-weaving.

As long as you invest in marketing and spend time researching your three categories, you will be in a great position to be #1 in at least one category for the best-selling author authority piece. Once you do hit #1 in at least one category then make sure you take a print screen of the sales ranking for social proof. I have been baffled when I have had prospective clients willing to pay up to eighty thousand dollars to be on *The Wall Street Journal* best-sellers list. Personally, I have witnessed that ninety-nine percent of our population does not care about the difference between the best-selling lists on Amazon, *USA Today*, or *The Wall Street Journal*. At the end of the day, hitting #1 is the main goal and you are able to use the best-selling author piece to promote your business and brand.

In this book, I have mentioned a few products that may help in your author journey. One thing I want to make clear is that there are no affiliate links in this book. I mention the products because I believe in them and use them myself.

My goal with this book is to help anyone who is looking to market their book successfully regardless of genre. The concepts I am covering have the potential to be a huge help when marketing your book both for the launch and beyond. Again, I never make any guarantees, but I can share with you what has worked for my books and our clients' books. With over one hundred best-selling launches, we have the track record to show that having a proven system can make a difference for your book.

CHAPTER 9
DEALING WITH AMAZON SALES RANKING DELAYS AND GLITCHES

Throughout this book, I have made multiple updates from the first and second edition to make this the most relevant and current book about book marketing that is available. I created this chapter update especially for the third edition of this book as this is in my view one of the biggest challenges with dealing with Amazon in 2023.

One of the things we have noticed during book launches over the past two years is the constant sales delays with the Amazon sales rankings. It started with a sales ranking delay of a few hours and then escalated into a multi-hour delay.

During a launch in December 2021, we had the biggest challenge yet. On December 7, 2021, there was a worldwide outage that halted Amazon to a crawl. On that day, you could not get onto the Amazon website for hours. When you finally got on the site, only parts of it were working.

This glitch almost destroyed a book launch for our client and put in danger our streak consecutive best selling book launches at that time. Not only did Amazon delay the sales rankings, they also did not even count those sales numbers towards the sales rankings. My client still received the royalties for the triple digit sales she had that day, but with the glitch, none of those counted towards the sales ranking.

Due to the glitch, my client did not hit #1 in any categories and Amazon did not care nor offer any solutions. I immediately created a backup plan as this affected many books that launched that week for authors across the world. What I am about to share with you should go a long way when considering if you should hire a company to manage your book launch.

I contacted several of my top book promo companies to come up with a solution. After many conversations, the consensus was that it was not the fault of the book promo companies because the client still got a lot of book sales, and the Amazon glitch was out of their control.

After hearing their side, I agreed that it was not their fault, but that I still needed to take care of my client. I asked them as a favor to me due to our long-standing business relationship to run the promos again exactly one week later so that we could take care of our client. In December, most book promo companies are fully booked throughout the month. The main thing I wanted was to get the results for my client and I agreed to pay for the promos once again in full as long as they could run the promos again the following week.

My client was not charged anything extra as it was not her fault. The book promo companies did not give me a discount as it was not their fault. I chose to pay for a brand-new set of book promos because we have a #1 best seller guarantee. That guarantee is our word that our client will hit #1 in at least one book category during the launch, and we were going to keep our word even if it was not our fault.

One week later, our client hit #1 in multiple categories, and she was very understanding of what happened. She was also thrilled that we went above and beyond to ensure that our client got the results she was looking for.

In December 2022, we had a similar issue, but it was worse. Amazon had a sales ranking glitch that lasted from the second week of December until the third week of January. It only hurt one of our launches as I decided to have our final launch of the year during the second week of December.

We ended up running the launch again for the client at the end of January and we got her to #1 in multiple categories. Due to the second consecutive year of having a major glitch in December, I decided that we would no longer launch books between Mid-November through the end of January each year.

These Amazon glitches are happening consistently during the holiday season, and we are no longer going to put our book launches at risk, especially when these factors are out of our control. Due to this issue, I no longer recommend that anyone launch a book between Mid-November through the end of January as there is no point putting your book launch at risk.

If you were marketing the book yourself then what would you have done? Could you have gotten those book promo companies to run your book promos again a few days later? In the case that you use a publisher or a book marketing service, would they have gone above and beyond to ensure that your book hit #1 or would then have said that it was not their fault?

These are the questions that you need to ask yourself in case you have an Amazon glitch when launching your book as it could happen.

CHAPTER 10
CREATING A
PRESS RELEASE

Should you end up hitting #1 in at least one book category, you will want to celebrate the achievement. For social proof, check your book's ranking on Amazon and then take a screenshot that shows you hit #1 during the paid phase of your launch. You can use the screenshot on your website or just keep it for your own records.

You should also consider writing a press release to celebrate your launch. We write press releases for client launches and then send the press release to our clients for approval. They will either ask for a few minor updates or approve the press release. Once the press release is approved, we send it over to the client in Word, PDF, and JPG.

We send the press release in JPG so clients can add it to their website and on their social media. They can also add it in an email to their list if they want to. I share this because you can do the same thing. The press release is mainly for you to promote your book, business, and brand. It is an additional authority piece for promotion.

Below is an example of how to create a press release.

Contact Name Paul Brodie   FOR IMMEDIATE RELEASE

Phone Number 469-323-6238

Email Brodie@BrodieConsultingGroup.com

Website BCGPublishing.com

Sheriff Launches Best-Selling Book

Arlington, Texas, December 2, 2020 – *American Sheriff* – written by Mark Lamb has just concluded a successful book launch on Amazon with the book ranked as a #1 Best Seller in multiple categories.

The book identifies and discusses what life is like as a county sheriff and how he has been forged by hardships, wins, and losses to rise above the challenges and lead from the front in law enforcement and in politics.

Sheriff Lamb also covers his core values of faith, family, love of country, courage, and perseverance.

"This is a great read! I love the part where Mark talks about going through a scary situation while living in South America as a teenager due to his father's employment. Having lived in Ecuador myself, I too remember extremely well the feeling of first

arriving back in the USA and hearing the words welcome home, which brought me to tears!"

- Sarah English

The book, published and marketed by BCG Publishing, is available on Amazon in Kindle and paperback formats.

Mark Lamb can be reached at AmericanSheriff.com for speaking opportunities.

###

Let's go through the press release areas assuming that you are publishing and launching the book yourself. The contact name needs to be your name. The phone number should be the best phone number to reach you. Add your email under email address and website for your website. You also need to put the words "For Immediate Release" on the right side.

Use a catchy headline. Think of the industry you're in. If you are a business coach, then the headline would be "Business Coach Launches Best-Selling Book." Another example is if you are a doctor, the headline would be "Doctor Launches Best-Selling Book." You want the headline to be simple with a clear objective, as in Mark's example.

Start the first sentence with the city and state where you reside currently, add the date of the press release followed by the name of your book, your name, and the fact that your book just concluded a successful launch on Amazon and is a #1 best seller in multiple categories. As another example, I would write the following:

Arlington, TX, July 5, 2021 – *Book Marketing Secrets* – written by Paul Brodie has just concluded a book launch on Amazon with the book ranked as a #1 Best Seller in multiple categories.

I will make the word "Amazon" a hyperlink to the book, which is something I also do for our clients.

The next sentence tells you more about the book. As an example, this is what I would add for *Book Marketing Secrets*: the book identifies how to market a book effectively and to maximize it as a lead generation tool for your business and brand.

Below that section, I would add a book review from my Amazon book page. On the next line you could mention the book is available on Amazon (include the hyperlink to your book page) in Kindle and paperback. On the final line you can mention that you can be reached at your website (include website link) for speaking and consulting opportunities.

The press release can be used for all genres. We have written multiple fiction press releases and always use the same format. The only difference is on the final line, where we mention that the author can be reached through their website (we include the website link) and that readers can join the author's email list or subscribe to their newsletter.

The press release is a great avenue to add authority for your business and author brand. You can also use it as a lead generation tool, as you are plugging your book and inviting the reader to connect further with you on your website. The press release is a tool that not enough authors use.

We only started using it as part of our book launch marketing service a few years ago and our clients love that we include it with their service. By using the framework in this chapter, you will be able to write a great-looking and professional press release.

CHAPTER 11
PLANNING A
PODCAST TOUR

Once the launch has concluded, you have the perfect opportunity to plan a podcast tour. Guesting on podcasts is one of the best ways to promote your book organically for the long term. It does take work and persistence, and in this chapter, I will show you several ways to get booked on podcasts for long- term book promotion.

Researching podcasts should be one of the first things you do after completing your book. Look at podcasts that cover topics related to your genre. Do Google searches on those podcasts and see if you can find more information about those shows.

Once you have found the shows that you would like to potentially be a guest on, subscribe to that podcast and listen to at least one or two episodes. Podcasts will either have guests or will be mainly solocasts, where the host is the one who is always talking. They may have a co-host, but they may not have guests.

That's why it is important to do research—this was one error I made a few years ago.

I reached out to a particular show that I felt was a great fit to promote my book, business, and brand. The only problem was that I did not do enough research into the show and did not listen to any of the episodes. After I sent out an email, I did not hear anything back.

One week later, I sent another follow-up pitching myself as a guest. The host responded within one day and asked if I even took the time to listen to his show. He mentioned that if I had taken the time to listen, I would have realized that he does not have guests on his podcast and that he is the only one who does the talking on his show.

It was not a pleasant message and it reminded me to always listen to at least one or two episodes before reaching out. Most podcasts have a website that either have a contact form or an email address where they can be reached. Doing due diligence in these areas is critical. Once you have found potential podcasts, listened to a couple of episodes, and have their contact info, then it's time to start your campaign of flattery.

The first thing to do is subscribe to the podcast. There are a ton of ways to get your podcast from iTunes to Google Play. I prefer to focus on iTunes because similar to Amazon, they generate most of the podcast traffic. After subscribing, listen to one or two episodes and then leave a five-star review for the podcast.

Now is the time to reach out to the podcast host for your campaign of flattery. In the initial email, mention that you are a huge fan of the podcast. You want to mention that you are a subscriber and recently left a five-star review for the show.

Mention a specific episode that you listened to and share a few things about why you loved the episode.

Once you establish the campaign of flattery, then mention that you would be honored to potentially serve as a guest on their show in the future. This is when you want to say that you have just published your first book and then tell the host three things that your book could help his/her audience with. Include a digital copy of the book (after it is edited) and tell the host once again how much you love the show and what a great honor it would be to serve as a guest in the future.

As a podcast host, the emails I am most likely to respond to are ones that flatter. If someone has told me they love my Get Published Podcast, subscribed to my podcast, left a five-star review, and are a fit for my audience, then I will book them. Being a podcast host is tough, and if you are doing something to help the show's metrics (subscribing to the show and leaving a five-star review), then I'll send a personal email response and thank you. Many other podcast hosts are the same, as we greatly appreciate subscribers and especially that you left a five-star review, and podcast reviews are just as important as book reviews, in my opinion.

If for some reason you do not hear back from the podcast host within a week, send another quick email. It doesn't have to be a long email, just mention that you wanted to follow up to see if they received your message, as you love their show. Sometimes podcast hosts get busy and do not always respond quickly.

Use this same process for all the podcasts you want to reach out to. Also be realistic about your expectations. It will not be easy to get on some of the larger podcasts because they are booked many months in advance. Look for podcasts in your genre and check to see how many reviews the show has. If the show has less than thirty reviews, they are going to be more likely to respond to your email, as they are still growing.

Our publishing company connects our clients with up to fifteen different podcasts that we have relationships with. The podcasts range from nonfiction, fiction, self-help, and health and wellness to military, leadership, faith-based, and business. We set up introductions with those shows, and our clients usually get booked on at least five to seven of the shows, as podcasters are always looking for guests. In addition, we also include a guaranteed booking for our clients on the Get Published Podcast.

I am asked often how I was able to build up a strong network of podcasts—many of them were guests on my Get Published Podcast. Another strategy you can use is what I refer to as the Trojan horse method. The catch is that you have to have your own podcast. Earlier in this book I mentioned how we use LinkedIn to book our guests. We used the Meet Alfred software and reached out to up to 200 people a day.

With the software and with LinkedIn Premium, I was able to do searches on people who had podcasts. I would send a connection request and invite them to be a featured guest on my podcast. We got a lot of bookings this way and built many relationships with other hosts. Many of those interviews resulted in me also getting the opportunity to be on their shows.

From that point we were able to build relationships, and I would ask if they ever looked for guests. Many of them always needed guests for their shows. I mentioned what I do with our book publishing company and asked if I could send guest referrals to them if they were a potential fit for their shows. The hosts loved this and we were able to create these relationships with over fifteen podcasts to whom I constantly send guest referrals.

If a podcast host responds to you and mentions there is a booking fee, do not pay them. This is something I'm strongly against. I have had the opportunity to be on many different podcasts and I refuse to pay money to be on a podcast. This is a disturbing trend that I have noticed has increased more over the past several years. It's also something that I refuse to do as a podcast host and will never charge one of my guests to be on the show.

Another way to get on podcasts is to use a service that was recommended by my friend, and fellow publisher, Marcy Pusey. The service is called Pod Match and you can get more information at www.PodMatch.com. For a monthly service fee, you can use Pod Match to connect with podcasts that you are interested in potentially being a guest on.

By using these methods and by being consistent and persistent, you should be able to get booked on a number of podcasts to promote your book for the long term.

CHAPTER 12
HOSTING A BOOK
LAUNCH PARTY

Everyone loves a party. As someone who has witnessed multiple book signings, I can tell you that hosting a book launch party is the way. In 2019, I launched a co-authored book called the *Get Published Business Book*. I had seventy-five co-authors in the book, many of whom resided locally here in the Greater Arlington area.

As part of the package, I mentioned that we would have a book signing party—besides being a lot of fun, it would be a great way to celebrate the book launch. Through a few networking connections, I was able to hold our book launch party at Texas Live, which is our new entertainment district in Arlington.

Texas Live is within walking distance of the Dallas Cowboys stadium and both the new and old ballparks for the Texas Rangers. One of the locations inside is a nice bar and restaurant, and I was able to book it for free. I booked it for a slow traffic day for the location, which was a Tuesday night when the Rangers were on the road. The management knew that we would be bringing in at least fifty people to the event, and they loved the idea.

It was a huge success. We had over fifty people in attendance and it was a lot of fun. I also created a program for the evening, and it became a template we use when advising our clients about their own book launch parties.

Six o'clock p.m. was the check-in time when all attendees would arrive and sign in. We set up a table in the front with two people who signed everyone in. On the form, we asked for their name, their business, phone number, and email address. You always want to get as much information as possible. We also had a fishbowl on the table and asked every attendee to put their business card in the fishbowl for a drawing for prizes at the event.

The check-in process went well and at 6:15, I started the event by welcoming everyone and thanking them for supporting our book launch party. Attendees were happy and ordering drinks and food, and we got started with the program. I walked them through the program and gave them details about the book, including how we had seventy-five people ranging from eight years old to eighty-two years old take part in the book. I shared their stories on topics like growing your business, building relationships, overcoming adversity, and the power of faith.

I then defined what a book launch party was. In addition, we were also having a book signing party in a couple weeks at the Greater Arlington Chamber of Commerce, and we plugged that event as well. At that point I introduced the general manager of Texas Live, who gave a brief presentation about the new venue.

The restaurant has a small stage and they gave us a microphone and speaker system to help us with the event. I was also able to have them put my company logo on every screen at the restaurant, and it was quite the visual. We had a banner created for the event and we had several sponsors ranging from a digital marketing company that livestreamed the entire event on Facebook for awareness, to a video producer who created a promo video of interviews with co-authors of the book. Our friends at 3DI-Sign + Design created a beautiful banner for the event with all of the sponsors on it, and we were able to use it as the background on the stage.

Another thing we did at the event was to host an author panel. I served as the Oprah of the panel and asked questions to six of our co-authors. I had our eight-year-old and eighty-two-year-old on the panel to create the connection with the age range, as well as two of my business mentors, the CEO of the Chamber, and a business coach. It was a great panel and was well received by the audience.

I asked each guest four questions:

Question 1: Tell us about your chapter.

Question 2: How did you create your chapter? (I.e., typed on the computer, dictated the chapter via audio recording, question and answer method.)

Question 3: What advice would you give to an aspiring author who wants to share their story?

Question 4: How do you feel now that you are a published best-selling author?

After question 4, I opened it up to the audience to see if they had any questions. To close out the panel, I asked if there were any final comments from our author panel.

The panel took thirty minutes and then we had our group picture taken. After the group picture, we gave away several door prizes chosen randomly from those who put their business cards in the fishbowl. Multiple gifts had been donated, from Texas Rangers tickets and wonderful coffee from Salters Bros. Coffee Roasters to amazing food from Prince Lebanese Restaurant. Additional gifts included a couple copies of the *Get Published Business Book*, a massage from True Balance Therapeutic Massage, and tickets from Timeless Concerts.

When we concluded the event, I took a moment to thank every sponsor who supported our event and explained how they helped us. Attendees raved about the book launch party for many weeks after the event. Our co-authors loved it and all had a great time.

The main point of having a book launch party is to celebrate your book. Restaurants are a great location to have them, and by finding a low traffic day, you can easily get a restaurant to offer to host your event.

CHAPTER 13
AMAZON ADS
FOR LONG-TERM
MARKETING

If you want to have long-term sales for your book, there are two ways to do so. The first one was covered when I showed you how to plan a podcast tour. The second option is to use Amazon Ads.

Amazon Marketing Services is literally the ultimate Tom Sawyer effect. I'm sure you are familiar with the story of Tom Sawyer. When I was a teacher, I used to have a multi-week unit about Tom Sawyer for my English as a Second Language students. One of the hooks to get my students' attention was asking them to identify and explain how Tom Sawyer was a hustler.

The best example in the story was when Tom got in trouble and had to paint the fence outside his house. Tom didn't want to paint the fence; this is similar to how many people hate marketing and having to pay to market an event.

Tom came up with an idea to make painting the fence look fun so that others would do his work for him. He went out of his way to make it look like so much fun that other kids in the neighborhood stopped by to see what he was doing. He said he was having a great time painting the fence and made it look so fun that the other kids wanted to paint the fence. Not only did Tom see this opportunity to get others to paint the fence for him, but he decided to earn some revenue with it.

He had the kids wanting to paint the fence so badly that they paid him. They either gave him toys or money for the privilege of painting that fence. Tom ended up sitting back, relaxing, and playing with his new toys while the kids all did the work, and the fence was painted quickly.

This is literally how Amazon gets you to pay for the privilege of marketing your book through their Amazon Marketing Services. You are paying for ads so Amazon will promote your book on their platform, and Amazon is getting a percentage of your royalties. It's frustrating to have to pay for the privilege, but it is a necessary beast.

In the past, I have spent a significant amount monthly promoting all of my books. When I started using Amazon Marketing Services in 2017, there was not a lot of competition. I found a service that would create all the ads for Amazon and I would give them a percentage of the royalties. At first, many of my books were highly profitable.

In 2017 and 2018, I made five figures in royalties each year thanks to Amazon Advertising. I would end up spending around five hundred dollars per month on advertising but would make a lot more in royalties.

Starting in 2019, there were more authors than ever who were advertising their books with Amazon Marketing Services. The market became bloated and there was a lot more competition. My profits were becoming less and less to a point where I parted ways with the agency I was using to advertise on Amazon.

At that point I managed the ads myself, but the results were not great. I was barely making a profit as we entered 2020. At that point, I removed my books from Amazon Advertising and focused more than ever on giving away copies of my *Get Published* book. In 2021, I started using Amazon Advertising again, but only with two books.

The first book was *Virtual Summit Secrets* and the second was *Book Marketing Secrets*. I work with Alex Strathdee at Advanced Amazon Ads and also refer clients to him as well for non-fiction books, as his core values align with mine. Alex studies Amazon Ads daily, and the advertising I have done with him has made a profit. As I am focusing on the back end with those books in particular, any profit is nice. His website is www.advancedamazonads.com if you want more information.

Alex markets books in mainly non-fiction. I am impressed with his systems-based approach. I also like that he stays current with the trends and is not afraid to try different things with ads. He has earned my trust and respect and that is why I mention this in the book, because if you need help, I highly recommend reaching out to Alex.

I also recommend Brian Berni to my children's book and fiction clients for Amazon Advertising and you can connect with Brian at https://bookads.co/.

You can track the profit margin of your books through a stat called ACOS (Advertising Cost of Sales) in the Amazon Marketing Services Dashboard. The lower ACOS you have, the better. During the 2021 Get Published Summit, I had three experts who spoke about Amazon Marketing Services: Brian Berni, Marc Reklau, and Alex Strathdee.

Brian and Alex both run Amazon Marketing Campaigns for their clients. Marc only runs ads on his own books and has generated hundreds of thousands of dollars in revenue for his books. I have studied Amazon Advertising myself and also bought Mark Dawson's Amazon Advertising course so that I could learn more about the process.

I suggest doing your research and if you want to do this yourself, check out Mark Dawson's Amazon Advertising course. If you are like me and want to outsource this, then I recommend reaching out to Alex at Advanced Amazon Ads.

CHAPTER 14
SECOND EDITION
BOOK LAUNCH

There is one final method that I recommend for marketing your book into the future. One of the services we offer clients is our second edition book launch marketing service. With this service we have our clients update their current book. Usually you only need to add around ten to fifteen percent new content. If you do not want to make updates with your book then you can also create an afterword chapter with the new content only in that section.

We also recommend creating a new book cover, but it is not necessary if you absolutely do not want to change your book cover. What we then do is update the book (and book cover if needed) and upload the book to Amazon as a new book. After Amazon sends the email that the book is now available on Amazon, we unpublish the original first edition, go into Amazon KDP, and send a message to the Amazon KDP department.

In the email we state that we just uploaded the updated second edition of the book and that we unpublished the original first edition. We ask Amazon to please transfer over the reviews and the book categories.

Within two days, Amazon will move over all the reviews and transfer the book categories to the second edition of your book. When you then go to your Amazon book page, you will see a new publication date, which will most likely be one day prior to when you uploaded the second edition. This means that you have a fresh start with your book.

You can literally treat the book like a brand-new book launch as it is the ultimate second chance. It will also be eligible to be considered part of the Amazon hot new release list for the first thirty days after the publication date. You have created some new content and now you have a second shot to market your book.

I started this method in 2018. In January 2016, I published my fourth book, *Book Publishing for Beginners*. It was my fourth best-selling book and sold well for a year and a half. By the end of 2017, sales slowed down, and I wanted to give it an update.

In January 2018, I updated the book with ten percent new content, had another great-looking book cover created, and went through the process I mentioned a few paragraphs ago. We launched the book again in late January 2018 and it hit the best-seller and hot new release lists once again.

It gave my old book a big push and we made sales and added new clients. Think of a second edition book launch as the equivalent of adding a new paint job to a car. It is well worth trying out.

You can also do it every three to six months—I know authors who have a fifteenth edition of their book. That may be a little excessive, but it shows how you can keep your book's momentum going; we have done many second edition launches for our clients.

CONCLUSION

The main things we have covered in this book include how you can use simple steps to market your book and to help you gain increased authority so that you can grow your business and position yourself as a subject matter expert. We also covered the three things you must have before your book launch.

We discussed how to optimize your book by having a lead magnet, website, and core offer. Those pieces are critical to your launch, as all three have a role in building your email list. Once you start building your email list, then you need to figure out your communication rhythm with your audience. I talked about how I email my list usually once per week at the same day and time. Additional emails are used when we are doing an affiliate promotion and I shared how you can as well, in order to add additional revenue to your monthly income.

In this book, we answered the question about whether social media helps with a launch. While it is great for awareness, we have seen little conversion for sales, and again this shows why having an email list is critical to the current and future success for your book, business, and brand.

We covered how to create a book launch marketing plan, the importance of getting reviews during upload week, and making sure everything is correct on your Amazon book page for the online launch week with the free and paid phases of your book. I also shared some of the book companies we use and how they can help with your launch, as their email blasts go to an engaged audience that will help with conversion for your book.

Having a launch plan is critical to the success of your book. Category research is another critical area, and I showed how you can search through over nineteen thousand categories through Publisher Rocket. I also showed how to find the categories in your genre that will help ensure that you hit #1 in at least one category during your book launch.

We then covered how to leverage your best-selling book by taking screenshots of the book hitting #1 and how to create a press release to celebrate your launch. The press release is ideal for your website and social media for exposure and for that authority piece of becoming a best-selling author.

Planning a podcast tour is one of the best ways to market your book organically for potentially months after your book launch. As part of the chapter, we showed how you can connect with podcast hosts in a way that will help you potentially get booked on those podcasts by supporting their show before you ask to be on it.

We wrapped up the book by showing you how to host a book launch party, get help with Amazon Ads for your book, and create a second edition book launch. We covered a lot of information, and by implementing the frameworks I have mentioned, the odds of having a successful book launch will greatly increase.

At this point you will either attempt to do this yourself or get help. However, if you want to work with me to market your book to be a #1 best seller through our proven system and to have someone as your personal guide, then I do invite you to set up a complimentary strategy session, which you can book in our next section. The main thing I want to know on the call is about your book and how you want to use it to grow your business and brand and to serve others in their journey.

The main point is that we want to help make sure your book has the greatest impact possible. If you do need additional support, then I strongly recommend that you book a complimentary session with me on the next page. I want to make clear that it is a no-pitch call. All I want to do is talk with you about your book and how we can potentially help you. I hope you enjoyed my book and found it valuable, and I wish you all the best in your author journey ahead.

STRATEGY SESSION INVITATION

I hope that you have enjoyed reading my book.

This was truly a labor of love, and it was an honor to help you in your journey to market your book.

If you would like to discuss getting help with your book, then we would love to talk with you.

In celebration of our nineteenth book, I would like to extend a personal invitation to you for a complimentary strategy session.

It is a no-pitch session—all we want to do is find out more about you and your potential book to see if we can help.

This is not a sales call.

Our only intention is to see if and how we can help you.

Due to time constraints, the call must be limited to fifteen minutes.

Are you ready to get started?

Go to www.BrodieConsultingGroup.com to book your complimentary strategy session today.

AFTERWORD

I decided to update this book into a third edition in May 2023. This was due to the many changes that happen in book marketing. The Amazon sales delay rankings also was an area I wanted to dedicate a new chapter to as it is becoming an issue during book launches that has hurt many authors.

These issues have even caused a Facebook Group to be created about how Amazon has ruined book launches. It is called Zon Tanked my Release and can be easily found by using the Facebook search engine. The group has over 260 people in it and there are many posts about horror stories with how Amazon has hurt their respective launches.

The Amazon sales delays caused us to adjust our book launch marketing system, which I mentioned in detail in our book launch chapter.

One of the biggest challenges with book marketing is staying on top of the trends as things change constantly. You also must be prepared in case there are sales delays in the rankings and especially as Amazon has had major issues in both December 2021 and December 2022.

This is why we have our BCG Guarantee that guarantees that your book will hit #1 in at least one Amazon category, and we do not stop until our clients hit #1. We have launched over 100 consecutive best selling books and we are able to guarantee this result for our clients.

No matter which direction you decide to go, make sure you have a strong plan for your book launch and always have a backup plan.

MORE BOOKS
BY PAUL

" Quick and inexpensive reads for self-improvement, a healthier lifestyle, and book publishing."

Twenty-one time best-selling author Paul Brodie believes that books should be inexpensive, straightforward, direct, and not have a bunch of fluff.

Each of his books was created to solve problems, including living a healthy lifestyle, increasing motivation, improving positive thinking, traveling to amazing destinations, starting a podcast, and helping authors get published, market a book effectively, share their story, and grow their business and brand.

What makes Paul's books different is his ability to explain complex ideas and strategies in a simple, accessible way that you can implement immediately.

Want to know more?

Go to www.BrodieConsultingGroup.com to check out Paul's books (available in Kindle, paperback, and audiobook formats).

ABOUT THE AUTHOR

Paul Brodie is a multi-time best-selling author and CEO of Brodie Consulting Group.

He helps medical professionals, attorneys, coaches, consultants, speakers, and business owners share their story with a proven system through book publishing and virtual summit creation.

What makes Paul's books different is his ability to explain complex ideas and strategies in a simple, accessible way that you can implement immediately.

Paul is a lifelong learner and earned an M.A. in Teaching from Louisiana College and a B.B.A. in Management from the University of Texas at Arlington.

In his spare time, he loves to read and write books, travel (especially to Maui and Las Vegas), and is an avid sports fan.

Paul is a proud Rotarian and holds membership in the Corporate Leadership Council of the Greater Arlington Chamber of Commerce. He also serves on the Board of Directors for the Rotary Club of Arlington Highlands, River Legacy Foundation, and the Greater Arlington Chamber of Commerce.

Paul resides in Arlington, TX and can be reached at Brodie@BrodieConsultingGroup.com and www.BrodieConsultingGroup.com for speaking, coaching, and consulting opportunities.

ACKNOWLEDGMENTS

Thank you to God for guidance and protection throughout my life.

Thank YOU, the reader, for investing your time reading this book.

Thank you to my amazing mom, Barbara Brodie, for all the years of support and a kick in the butt when needed.

Thank you to my awesome sister, Dr. Heather Ottaway, for all the help with and feedback on my books and with my motivational seminars. It is scary how similar we are.

Thank you to my dad, Bill "The Wild Scotsman" Brodie, for his encouragement and support with the business aspects of Brodie Consulting Group.

Thank you to my good friend and collaborator, Ray Brehm. You have taken our virtual summits to the next level and your friendship and knowledge is greatly appreciated.

Thank you to Bryan Acosta and Ruben Duarte. You both are like brothers to me, and it is great to serve with you both on multiple local boards for the Arlington community.

Thank you to all the amazing friends I have worked with over the past thirty years. Each of you has made a great impact on my life.

Thank you to Delta Sigma Pi business fraternity. I learned a great deal about public speaking and leadership through the organization, and every experience I have had helped me become the person I am today.

Thank you to my three best friends: J. Dean Craig, Jen Mamber, and Aaron Krzycki. We have gone through a lot together, and I look forward to many more years of friendship.

CONTACT
INFORMATION

Paul can be reached at Brodie@BrodieConsultingGroup.com

Website: BrodieConsultingGroup.com

Publishing and coaching services:
BrodieConsultingGroup.com/services

Media: BrodieConsultingGroup.com/media

Get Published Podcast: GetPublishedPodcast.com

Join our Get Published Facebook Group

Follow Paul on Instagram

Follow Paul on Twitter: @GetPublished

Like Paul's author page on Facebook

Connect with Paul on LinkedIn

FEEDBACK REQUEST

Please leave a review for our book, as I would greatly appreciate your feedback.

If for some reason you did not enjoy the book, then please contact me at Brodie@BrodieConsultingGroup.com to discuss options prior to leaving a negative review, and please feel free to let me know how the book can be improved.